Malcolm May

Tale Publishing

First Published 2019
Copyright © 2019 Malcolm May
All right reserved.
ISBN- 978-0-6483273-7-0

National Library of Australia Cataloguing-in-Publication entry:
Author: Malcolm May
Illustrator: Magdalena Almero Nocea
Produced+Editors: Don May + Elizabeth Symonds
Title: The Good Old Days in Gippsland/ Malcolm May

Tale Publishing
Melbourne Victoria

Cover image: This giant mountain ash 11 metres in diameter and 34 metres in circumference, was cut down around 1900, near the corner of the Grand Ridge Rd and Cooks Rd at Balook, Victoria.

Author contact via: WarwickGardensOlinda@gmail.com

Ebook available on Amazon.com

Printed in Australia

Australian bush poetry

Malcolm May

Malcolm grew up on a farm at Won Wron and attended State School in 1944 during and after the Second World War. Times were tough, what with the drought, rabbit plague, limited finance and being number four in a family of seven. We survived on home grown hand me downs but above all a sense of humour. The farm was situated between the state forest on the east and a large swamp on the west which was full of snakes plenty of wild ducks and native fish. We lived off the land, for pocket money us kids trapped rabbits for 40 cents a pair, foxes 75 cents from which I earnt more money than my teacher. I left school at 14 to become a Mr fixit at the local garage for 3 years. My next job was before I was 18, as a road contractor for the Country Roads Board (CRB). Over the years I always tended to write verses about aspects of my life's adventures.

Magdalena Almero Nocea

Magdalena grew up in Seville, Spain, belonging to a family that shared her love of the arts and provided her with unconditional support. Magdalena's passion for art, heritage and especially painting, led her to dedicate her life's work to them. She studied Fine Arts, with a major in painting and photography at the University of Seville. Following completion of her studies, Magdalena began working as a full time artist - creating illustration, book covers, portraits and advertisements because her dream is to be a small part of yours.

The Good Old Days in Gippsland

Written by Malcolm May

Illustrated by Magdalena Almero Nocea

Lead by Example

If you lead by example
To help someone else along
Give them a hand up
When they are not going strong.

If you're playing sport
You must turn the other cheek
To be a good loser
That people want to meet.

As you go through life
Some fall along the way.
They will be rewarded
If you pass the time of day.

To pick them up and urge them on.
And lend a helping hand.
You will give encouragement
To make another stand.

You don't have to be the P.M.
To get the people to believe
By being a role model
And wanting to achieve.

Sometimes you're under pressure
And wonder where you're wrong
Perhaps a sense of humour
Would keep things going strong.

When you're out there
And can help the world along
By setting a good example
To show where we belong.

Now we are all just "Aussies"
It's time to make a stand.
For we remain united
In this Sun burnt land.

The Drought of 68

It was a drought to remember
The drought of '68
There was more feed on the road
Than was inside the gate.

We moved our stock beyond the hills
All the way to Middle Creek.
Along those winding roads
With the country very steep

Travelling through Balook
Then passed the valley view
To flat country farmers
This was something new.

Down past Calder Junction
On this winding track
With our hundred head of cattle
Before nightfall had time to unpack.

For 3 months in this valley
With its pasture lush and green
To see the cattle gain condition
Was a picture to be seen.

When the winter closes in
Will be anybody's guess
Thanks to the great attention
From the Reid family we will bless.

We headed back to Won Wron
All in fine condition
Walking all the way behind
Was another proposition.

Our feet were soon weary
And our knees began to knock
But thanks again to the Reid's
They helped us to the top.

We pushed on to Balook
We stopped there for a 'blow
Halfway through the night
Well, did it snow!!

When we got down to the flats
We made another count.
And to our discovery
Did not have the right amount.

So to Fred and company
Jack Rogerson and Burge
Victor Felmingham etc
We soon compiled the herd

Disregard the losses,
The worst of the weather
All the world we could have travelled
For friends were never better.

Dozers for Hire

The advert in the local "rag" this week
Read: some dozer drivers we do wish to speak.
They lined up to the office door
Long ones, short ones, fat ones by the score.

We sent them out to Mack's Creek
To a lonely range.
Some took a look and I could see
Their gizzards going strange.

Yes some of them progressive
But without a brain
They could turn the dozers over
Even out there on the plain

Another one religious
And did a little toil
But that silly fool
Ran the tractor out of oil.

There were other tractors.
The D7, it was slow
They were always fixing it'
Even when it snowed.

A new D6, it looked real good
Its performance, it was grand.
There was a poor old Alice Charmers
And its driver came from wonderland.

The other tractor is a Japanese job
You orter hear its motor throb.
Up and down the hills it goes
Better than all the other you know.

The moral of the story is
If a driver you must train
It's no darn good just coaxing him
You have to educate his brain

So we do not pay big money
To these skiting lads
So we must have a demo
Or we will end up being had.

I can listen to you bumkins
And skiting all you like
For I am heading homeward
Before you rot my tripe

The Barry Way

I'll take you on a trip where the Snowy River rises
Past the Koscuisko mountain that reaches to the sky.
From Kiandra, you pass Lake Eucumbene,
Trout fishing is the best you have even seen

At the showpiece town of Jindabyne
Take the time to view a cattle sale.
100 years ago the stock were driven
From the mountains to the Bairnsdale rail.

This stock route is known as the Barry Way,
Named after Leo Barry, who locals had respect.
Through the national park, past Craigies lookout
This was the shortest journey as it was direct.

You leave behind the High Plains
With its mountain peaks
Down this winding road, called Jacobs Ladder
You drop two thousand feet.

Along the Snowy River,
White pines and tall poplars stand supreme
On the river banks, purple violets, kings cups
Are pictures to be seen

When you're at the Victorian border
There are name plates on a rock
About the men who drove their cattle
And that time forgot.

At the Suggan Buggan
The old school house is a prize.
The pistachio nut farm
Is on the Northern rise.

Climbing up to Black Mountain
The rock face by the road is sheer
You see rock wallabies leap from rock to rock.
They need another gear.

Out on the Cobbler Mountains
Where the brumbies, they run free,
Mountain ponies with their flowing manes,
It's a vision just to see.

At the little River the water falls 1000 feet
Down the rock walls of the narrows
To McKillops Bridge is where
The water dragons you can meet

When you pass through Walgulmerang
Then to Glenantipy
The view is from the mountains
Down there to the sea.

Whilst down in Buchan
You must see the caves
View the fossils in the rocks
And wonder at their age.

First came MacMillan, an explorer
With Charlie Tarra as his guide.
By the Dargo Road
Where Angus MacMillan died

In 1840's the first settlers came to stay
Like the O'Rourke's at Bruthen Creek
They drove their bullock drays
And brought along their sheep.

When you travel on this road
Where wonders never cease
200 years ago you would only
Be walking on your feet.

On Australia Day we pause to remember
Our pioneers of long ago
Thankful of the folks around us
And all the people that we know.

Callignee School Race 1981

Working on the road that leads down to Loy Lang
It has been marvellous that there's never been a prang
I've just commenced my work, with my grader and my truck,
For it is my endeavour to make an honest buck.

Life has been a nightmare down Callignee way
For it is no wonder my hair is growing grey.
The teacher has arrived on her Suzuki motor skate.
She has begun to put the writing on the slates.

The way these mums drive to get their kids to school
To stay alive on this road is a job for no ordinary fool
I hear a mighty roar that sounds like Peter Brock,
It's like a warning bell that it is almost 9 o'clock

First appears on the scene is a little diesel red machine
She roars around each corner, the kids are looking green
She drives like it was a truck, you'd think it was my Mack
Going by the smoke that's coming out the back

Judging by the hair do, she had her finger in the electric jug
Or perhaps she's been fiddling with a 3 pin plug.
Gwenda in the race, she gave a cow a rumble,
Going by the kids description they nearby did a tumble

The kids have all arrived at school safety do not mention
Teacher has got them all lined up, standing at attention.
The women all head homeward bound to wash the pots and pans
Then its out onto their back lawn to add to their suntan.

Now all you lead footed women, if you really want a rally
I would invite you down to Tarra Valley.
For my wife she's got a "Kenworth" in it's a dirty great "GM"
And it will be "God help you" if you meet her on the bend.

When she's heading down hill, you can smell the burning brakes
I tell you it's not safe, even for a tiger snake.
When the dust is settled, the kids have gone to bed
If you have not got a sense of humour you might well be dead.

In my roadwork job, you can have a little fun
Now I see approaching the end of 81.
In this little verse I have had a little jest
For it is almost Christmas I wish you all the very best.

Wonnangatta Adventure

A little note to Jack and Arthur Guy.
Of a trip we thought we would like to try
Heading off with mum, and the kids too
Things were going nicely without a single blue

Calling at your sister, Mrs Randell
The crooked road the landrover would handle
Tell that lad "young Alex Trail"
After several miles we were going pale.

Up and down through wombat range
The country was surely strange.
When we got to Wangaratta
We found there was no-one atta

Leaving there the vermin was so thick
I could have killed them with a stick.
After leaving the old stockyard
The track started to get hard

It set in and did it rain
Heading up to Howitt Plains
Going upward in the flood
The track churned up into mud.

We got out to push up some hills
This is where the trip lost its thrills.
When we made it to the top
The track had become a flaming slop

With a bloomin lot of luck
We made it to the "Howitt Hut"
We met some of your splendid stock
I would not mind them in my flock.

We spent the night by open fire
The next day it was a heavy fog
Now we are off to Traralgon
People, cars and oh the smog.

Now down in the valley it was dry as hell
Of your fine pasture I will surely tell.
With all your mountains and fine stock
It's a place all should make a stop

The Bower Bird

The bower bird when at his best,
Will work all day and never rest.
Gathers sticks from miles around,
Plants them firmly in the ground

A bird built bower made for play
Such a work of art.
Gathered are the trinkets on display
With such beauty to impart.

A blue eyed bird with building rare
The dancing bird with so much flair.
To attract a female partner there
The bower bird to see or compare.

Blue trinkets that you do not keep
A blue tag he would steal
He gave the surroundings such a hue
For everything he painted blue.

The musk and wattle too
It was part of his play,
He'd paint and daub til all went blue
Til the blue bag wore away

No other bird with such skill
Than the bower bird with satin sheen.
Gathering berries to his larder fill
Attracts his mate with mottled green.

Along with pebbles
To his bower store
And lay around his dancing floor.
His scheme is something to implore.

Australian birds are quite unique
Where visitors' they come to seek
To watch our birds at their play
In the bush we see this every day.

The Little Country Hall

On those rolling hills
Where the gum trees grow tall
At the lonely crossroads
Stands remnants of a little country hall.

With its creaking doors and rusty spout
Where once they held a ball
Now the population has moved out
And left behind their little country hall.

Where people used to gather
Children went to school.
They learnt to salute the flag
That was the normal rule.

We always help each other
When the going was real tough
In fire or floods and famine
To get out of the rough.

When I visit this far country
Walk within its rustic walls.
I wonder of the memories
In that little country hall.

If you walk through life
Wonder where the time has gone
But in a few more years
A new life will be born.

As I drive this country road
Where wildflowers are supreme
Of my childhood memories
I can only dream.

In that country hall
Where I first met my wife.
Of those great memories
As I walk through life.

The piano it was rocking
But a little out of tune
And everyone was happy
At the sight of a full moon.

In those passing years
It will be someone else's call
To wonder of the memories
In that little country hall.

A Fair Dinkum Aussie

If you want to be a fair dinkum Aussie
It starts when you fall from the cot
About wanting part of the action,
Whether you are ready or not.

Don't start pinching their lollies
Or pulling someone's hair
If you get bad tempered
You may fall off your chair.

Seize every moment
When you are going off to school
It's all about a good education
And not acting the fool.

If you want job satisfaction
You must have a smile on your face
Treat everyone as your equal
To win respect in the workplace.

Think about the big picture
If you desire to achieve
Be ready to get started
And wanting to believe

When you say that you are an Aussie
Look them straight in the eye
Give them a hand shake
And they know you are dinky-di.

Aussies are full of inventions
And bursting with brains
We like straight talkers
When they are trying to explain.

When you meet someone
Always pass the time of day.
Help some distant traveller
To go upon his way.

For life is a journey
With many weary miles
Sometimes you can help
Just with a kind smile.

Now I am growing older
And it is time to take a rest
To watch the next generation
To achieve at their best.

Down on the Farm

Thought I'd write a verse
About when I was just a kid
How we all survived
And how we made a quid.

We were a big family
For we numbered nine in all
But when it came to fun
We really had a ball.

For breakfast we had porridge
That was really thick
Charging up our batteries
Eggs on toast did the trick.

Each of us had jobs to do
Feed the chooks or catch the horse
To get us off to school
Father had to reinforce.

Teacher had to work real hard
To get something in our brain
But when he got frustrated
Would start smoking like a train.

Homeward bound from school
I would reset my rabbit traps
Change my clothes, untie the horse
And remove him from his straps.

Feeding calves with buckets
Fill up the old wood box
Collect the eggs, lock up the chooks
To keep them from the fox.

We knew about organics
In our vegie garden plots
We grew everything
Corn, carrots, onions and shallots.

World war two was dragging on
And everything was rationed
There were no lollies in the shops
Clothes were out of fashion.

Things had brightened up
Soldiers had returned from war
A new area had woken up
And god knows what's in store.

I'd be up in the early morning
When the birds start to sing
Weather has brightened up
At the first signs of spring.

Bees are gathering honey
And returning to their hives
Observe nature that surrounds you
You will really feel alive.

In the summertime we'd go fishing
Pick blackberries along the creek
After first rain in autumn
Mushrooms were a treat.

Take notice all you greenies
Go and plant a tree
You will be sustainable
For all the world to see.

For some people the world ends
At the bottom of the street
Come up to the bush sometime
We are friendly lot to meet.

My bones they are just aching
But my mind is crystal clear
I've been on the farm
For nearly eighty years.

I'm glad the devil does not know me
He'd have me stoking up his fire
I've got other plans to complete
Before I will retire.

I Met A Man One Day

I met a man one day, a real true blue Aussie bloke
Come and have a cuppa, hear a story or tell a joke.
Life's experiences interesting to behold
So many stories I have since been told,

He is nearly eighty years of age, a full life he has lived
A close and loving family, enjoys time spent with his grandkids.
He cares for his community, anyone who needs help
Raises money, mows lawns, whatever is bid.

His weathered old Akubra has seen the worse for wear
The old blue flannel shirt is letting in the air
Scuffed old R M Williams boots, they have had their day
The wise old man, his greying hair, his name is Malcolm May.

He earned his first pennies trapping rabbits and selling fox skins,
Feed the chooks, grow the veggies, school was not his thing.
Fishing for trout, picked blackberries along the creek,
After first rain in autumn mushrooms were a treat.

Bees are gathering honey and returning to their hives
Observe nature that surrounds, you will really feel alive.
Survived through WW II, everything was on ration
No lollies in the shops, clothes were out of fashion

He owned his first truck at 18 years of age
Soon to be working, earning a good wage
Met his little lady, decided to ask her for her hand.
Soon to be married with children and bought his own land.

Trucked in dirt and rock, built roads and many a bridge
He knows his way around Strezelecki and the Grand Ridge
Worked in the plantations, fought fires, floods and drought
His love for this our country is never in doubt.

Our great country he went to see, our unique forgotten past
Devil's Marbles, Uluru, Sandhill's, spinifex and regions vast
Rock art and fossils, gemstones east of Alice Springs
Opals, sapphires, diamonds, a land of many things

Mozzies as big as planes, Bathurst burr and bindii,
Dingoes, goats, and camels, buffalos and crocodile
When the heat of the day is spent, stop and have a beer.
An outback pub is where you can have some camaraderie

He showed me Tarra Valley, waterfalls cascading down the rocks
Groves of vines and creepers, tree ferns, and the superjacks
Orchids, clematis, myrtle, sassafras, mountain ash and beech
Hidden in the little valleys, to most people far out of reach.

We found footprints in the sand of Kangaroo and wild deer,
Though we never saw them, we knew that they were near
Stop and listen to the birds singing, listen to the bush,
The wind, the rain, the animals, the rivers as they rush.

We found a higher peak, many colours to be seen
A kaleidoscope of nature shades of blues and green.
Flowers and the fungi, reds and orange and gold
You must take time to look to see what will unfold

Now he has retired, memories and stories to tell,
About life and this land that he knows all too well.
I stop and have a cuppa, and you should too,
Always something to learn, as sure as the sky is blue.

To Malcolm and Margaret May,
A huge thankyou I want to say
You welcomed me to Yarram
This town I hope to stay.

-Wendy Helms

Gippsland

We live in this country called Gippsland
It reaches from the mountains to the sea.
With all of the natural beauty,
Oh, what a place just to be.

Years ago the railway came to Gippsland,
It gave access to large tracts of land.
Today they milk cows by the hundreds,
The products are on world demand.

We are lucky to have all these assets
Like the oil in Bass Strait.
It keeps the home fires burning
Oh what a wonderful place.

We have two very large sawmills
With many people employed.
For the country has prospered
With enrichment they have enjoyed.

The railway has long departed
Our lifeline is the "Hyland Way"
The government has granted millions
To get repairs under way.

I walk down the streets of Yarram
Remember the things I used to see
Then I let my memories wander
About how our lives used to be.

When you next come to Yarram
You must partake of the Country Club.
To reminisce your good memories
Remember how we survived in the scrub.

For your life is a journey
Make welcome whoever you meet
You will be rewarded
Next time you pass in the street.

Australia Day

You think we don't care
With all those nationalities
That has come to join us
In this country that we share.

For those that do oppose us
Are just a few percent.
They learn as they grow older
And show more common sense.

What's wrong with this great country?
That you want to spoil.
For our ancestors worked hard
Defending as they toiled.

Our aboriginal neighbours
I am first to recognise.
Everyone on this land
Has a right to survive.

Teach us to be compatible
Working together is our strength.
Uniting is what it is all about
Dividing has no sense.

Let us pull together
Put your shoulder to the wheel
Before some of those stirrers
Our human rights repeal.

You would expect better
From our leaders at the top
And not to promote
This underlying rot.

We are Australian

Come in and shut the door
And let us have a yarn
Tell us what you have done
Since you sold the farm.

We come from different walks of life
Because we don't do things by halves
Some other guys have been before
Being time poor makes me laugh

It doesn't matter what your colour
White, brindle, brown or black
Whilst we live together
There will be no going back

Don't bite the hand that feeds you
Or start looking for a fight
There's no reward in bullying
If you want to sleep at night

As Australians we are not racist
And mateship is essential
If this country is to achieve
And reach its full potential

When there is fire or flood
An Aussie always lends a hand
To help some weary person
Get back onto the land

What hazards come before us
We take them in our stride
Now we stand together
For as Australians we have our pride

When you say you are Australian
It really makes me proud
Whether you are at the football
Or mixing in a crowd.

Now you are always welcome
Throughout the country mate
We look forward to meeting again
At a later date.

I Remember When

I remember the years of my childhood.
When I lived upon the farm,
Where we often wandered for miles
But never came to harm.

When the milk came from the cow,
With an inch of cream on top.
All vegies came from the garden
Not from a supermarket shop.

As kids we played together
Cricket with a ball and stick.
Out in the back paddock,
That's where we got our kicks.

I remember going to markets
Where the cattle they were sold.
After to the shops
For pills for my cold

Toilet paper was from newspaper
The print stuck to your bum
It was hung upon a nail
A novelty for a new chum.

The dunny was down the back
In the dead of night I wished for a flame
But when you're in a hurry
There's no time to complain.

Clothes were boiled in a copper
With chopped up velvet suds.
Irons by the fire were never hot enough.
To remove all the wrinkles from your duds.

We never had an ice chest
Food was put down the well.
Home-made bread was crusty.
With jam and cream as well.

I got the strap across my backside
Soap for dinner if I swore.
A number ten to my bum
To even up the score.

There is fragrance in the flowers
And everything that grows.
And with the sweet music
In every breeze that blows

I think my memory is failing
And the nights are getting cold
Perhaps it's the first signs
Of me getting old

The Outback

Out there in outback Australia
It takes guts to stay alive
There is no-one else for miles around
It's a battle to survive.

Fire, insect plagues and dust storms
Monsoons, drought and flooding rains
You only have to wait a few years
It will all happen once again.

At night there is no one else around
It's too far to walk around the block
The only thing that will attack you
If you fall off your horse and hit a rock.

Bathurst burr and bindii,
Mossies as big as aeroplanes
Those things you take for granted
Power poles and water mains.

Dingoes, goats and camels
Are part of the outback scene
They cause so much destruction
You can see where they have been

Wild pigs are in the waterholes
Contaminating, spreading disease
When the other animals come to drink
They get bogged up to their knees.

Distance is no problem
In this Never Neverland
Don't forget to pack a swag
A well filled water bag.

Take a drive to Uluru
And view the old Ayers Rock
In the distance is Mt Connor
What a contrasting shock.

Australia has its many features
Oil mining agriculture and parks
Sandhill's, spinifex and regions vast
Unique to this country's forgotten past.

Rock art and fossils
Gemstones east of Alice Springs
Devils Marbles by the highway Craters
and other things.

At an outback pub
When the heat of the day is spent
You can have some camaraderie
Have a beer and repent.

Now as the years roll by
In this timeless land
As caretakers of this country
It's time to make a stand.

Of Home I Tell

Against a blue horizon the Strezelicki Ranges lie
There was once grew a great rainforest that reached up to the sky.
These solitary giants took a century to grow
Some of these I guess, girthed forty feet or so.

They grew with towering splendour through fire, gale and snow
But this was soon disrupted by the axemen and his blow.
Thanks to some wise person with a preserving thought in mind
Today is left a sample of what the axeman left behind.

Down a fern clad valley where it is very dark
It brings memories of a place called Bulga Park.
The township that was adjoining was known as Balook
And on the hill a school house stood.

The numbers there were forty or even forty four
But when the wind was blowing it nearly blew you out the door.
The folks that all lived there had a great spirit good and true
In the early days the log trucks rumbled through.

Down the Mack's Creek valley steam rose above the fog
There was a big contraption that winched up every log.
To the north a sawmill that perched above the bluff
It was owned by a good fellow by the name of Billy Duff.

There was another fellow by the name of Sammy Wills
He was a good axeman, the best in all the hills.
Patterson's and Sutton's were among the other boys
They had their little troubles like the Martins and the Coy's.

The big house was known as Grand Ridge Farm
I tell you when you were there they took you by the arm.
It was owned by the Campbells and their bunch of skinny kids
Mum and Jack had patience or they would have flipped their lids.

In a distant valley there was a farm called Hazel Dell
It over looked Mount Tassie as far as I can tell.
The Davis family owned it they milked a cow or two
They stick together just like blooming glue.

Their late father was a corporal I am told
And their mother had a heart of gold.
They had three lads and a girl that dabble in some strife
But this little lady has ended up my wife.

Now as the sun sinks lower around the end of the day
Through a ray of sunshine the wildlife come out to play.
As I close my eyes and remisise
There is not one day that I would ever miss

Been Around Australia

We have been around Australia
Done a mile or two
Had a few strong debates
But never had a "Blue"

I've got a good old Nissan
It has travelled many miles
Been across Australia
Done it all in style.

With the van hooked on the back
You can go just anywhere
Stop at a moment's notice
Light a fire and enjoy the air.

We have been around Australia
Up and down the coast
The old faithful camp oven
Can even cook a roast.

Through the middle to Alice Springs
Around the McDonald Range
Wander around the gem fields
We could do it all again.

Been to Mt Connor
Climbed to the top of Ayers Rock
Drove around the Olgas
Budgerigars in a hundred flock

Going up through Tennant Creek
Drive to Edith Falls
Enjoy a swim in the river
Aboriginal art on the rock wall.

Devils Marbles by the highway
You wonder how they got there
Next we go to Katherine
At a wayside stop we share.

When you're in the outback
You have to camp in the scrub
At times you meet some characters
Having lunch at Daly Waters Pub.

Katherine Gorge is worth a look
You can lunch upon the boat
Then swim in the hot spring,
Or on your Li-Lo float.

When we get to Pine Creek
The war cemetery you must see.
Hundreds in the war were killed
From Darwin who could not flee.

You must go to Kakado
Jabiru and Arnhem Land
Crocodiles in the rivers
The waterlilies on Fogg Dam.

When you are in Darwin
There are many things to see
Having dinner on the wharf
Admire the view of the Timor Sea.

Cullen Bay is a must to see
When the boats go in and out
With its opening gates
Protection from cyclones and water spouts.

Doctors Gully, you feed the fish
Visit Mendell Beach Bazaar.
Many other features to explore
When driving in your car.

The big tunnels under the city
Where to store diesel fuel
So the Japanese could not bomb
This was done to rule.

I'll go back to Katherine
Then across to the West
We will cross the Victoria River
From the heat will have a rest.

To the Western Australian border
Inspectors check for cane toads
Take away the vegies and honey'
Then you can hit the road.

After miles turn into Ord River Dam
A park overlooking Lake Argyle
Visit the Durack Homestead
Take a boat trip and stay a while.

Kununurra they grow sandalwood,
Sugarcane makes the best rum
You must not overindulge
Could end up on your bum.

Everyone who goes to the west
Must see the Bungle Bungles.
Hills look like marble cake
Red grevilleas are like a jungle

To the west there is Tunnel Creek
Inside the hill is a waterfall.
Walking two hundred metres
There is a window through the wall.

When you're at Winjana
Crocodiles on the river bank
Rows of red bottle brush
Rainbow birch on every branch

When you're at Derby
Big ore trucks come and go
Pulling five big trailers
Weighing one hundred ton or so.

On the eighty mile beach
Good fishing from the shore
The exotic shells wash up
They are spread galore.

When you're at Port Hedland
Twenty ore carriers waiting at sea
Ore trains two miles long
On the road that is blocking me.

Then we go to Exmouth
And visit Coral Bay
Continue on to Carnarvon
One week plan to stay.

It is so windy
You would not believe
Trees grow at a right angle
Lucky to keep their leaves.

There is a lot of market gardens
Gascoyne river is upside down
Irrigation water pumping
From underneath the ground

You can go to Monkey Mia
But we have seen porpoises before
Down there at Port Albert
Right at our back door.

We by-passed Perth
Headed for Hyden and Wave Rock.
Must see this curving rock
With its reservoir on top.

When driving this country
Many families of wild flowers.
It makes the journey interesting
To while away the hours.

Now we're down in Esperance
There's a big ship in the bay
With all the islands out to sea
What a wonderful display.

Heading up to Norseman,
Then across the Nullarbor
Watch out for the camels
Don't want one of them aboard.

For two days on the Nullarbor
You look out to the right
View the big grey whales
In the Great Australian Bight.

The Nissan still running nicely
As we wear away the miles
Pull in at Ceduna
There we stay a while.

Then we go to Cowell
In our boat whiting and squid
This will supplement our budget
It will save us a quid.

We travel to Port Augusta
Where all roads meet.
Where you cross Spencers Gulf
At the end of the main street.

We will go through Morgan
Murray River at Waikerie
Travel through the Riverland
Pick fruit straight from a tree.

Renmark it comes next
We cross into good old Vic.
Stop the night in Mildura
So many caravan parks to pick.

Down to Bendigo
Where once they dug for gold
I need to put my woollies on
I'm starting to feel the cold.

Now we are back in Gippsland
It's quite another scene
My neighbours want to know
"Where the devil have you been?"

Printed in Australia
AUHW010916031019
318138AU00001B/1

9 780648 327370